❧ NOBODY ❧ ASKED YOU

More Vintage Ladies Talking Trash

ADULT COLORING BOOK

Original unaltered images are from the British Library
on-line collection of public domain images found at:
www.flickr.com/photos/britishlibrary

instagram

Post coloring pages on instagram @colormenaughtybooks
#saltybitches

OTHER BOOKS BY COLOR ME NAUGHTY

 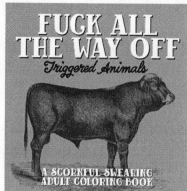 

AND

A CUP OF CHIC

NOBODY ASKED YOU

LISTEN TO
MY OPINIONS

GO POLISH YOUR CROCS

SALUTATIONS
MOTHERFUCKER

LET ME TELL YOU A STORY
FUCK YOU
THE END

INTEREST LEVEL
ZERO

KINDLY FUCK OFF

THANK U, NEXT

DROP DEAD FUCKFACE

PLEASE GOD, MAKE THE ASSHOLES DISSAPEAR

PLEASE LEAVE

GRL PWR

OUTFIT IS SNATCHED

FEELIN' MYSELF

GIRL
SQUAD

GUCCI

FARO
LAMBIC

SORRY FOR NOTHING

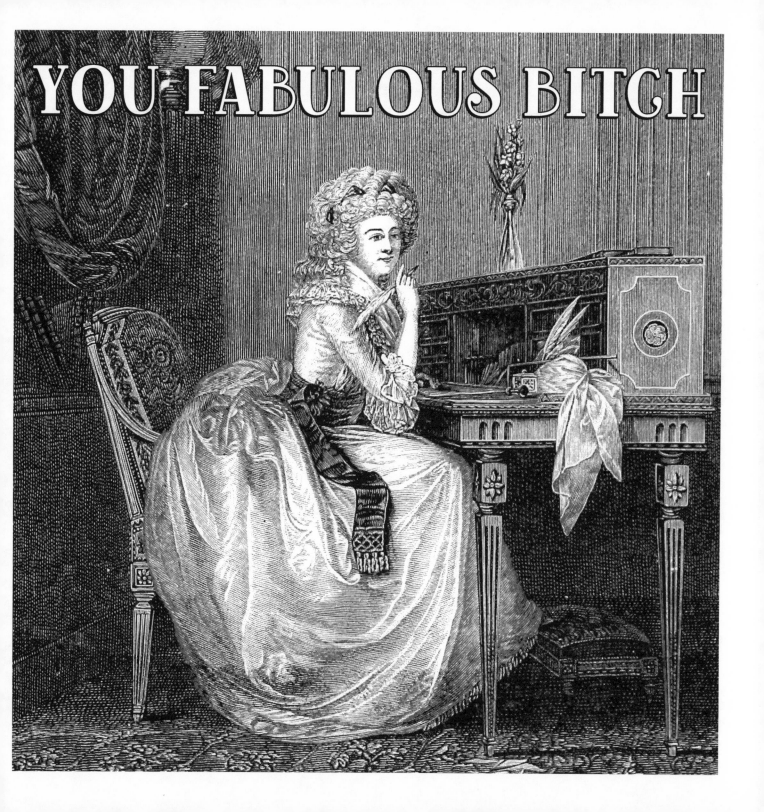

STAY OUT OF MY SHIT

THINK HARDER
MOTHERFUCKER

LEVEL UP

100% BABE

I'M NOT A LOOK
I'M A FEELING

GOOD VIBES

SALTY

DO NOT FUCK
WITH ME TODAY

PISS LORD OF
SHIT MOUNTAIN

STAY
HYDRATED

FLY AS FUCK

DON'T HOLD
YOUR BREATH

EAT SHIT

I'M LIVING FOR IT

GAME ON BITCHES

I HAVE FEELINGS TOO

HIGH KEY EMOTIONAL

SHUT IT SLUTBAG

YOU OLDE FUCKER

YOU INSUFFERABLY
SMUG SHITBAG

ADULTING IS SHIT

IT'S CALLED FINESSE
ASSHOLE

DO NOT FUCK
WITH NANA

100% TRASH

CALM YOUR TITS

Made in the USA
Coppell, TX
06 December 2022

87959537R00062